To Emmy, my dear friend, and to Barbara, my inspiration —L.C.

For David —R.J.

Grateful acknowledgment to Two Oceans Aquarium
for their permission to use the map of Yoshi's journey,
and to Jean Tresfon for the photo of Yoshi.

With this publication, Random House Children's Books has made
a donation to Two Oceans Aquarium's sea turtle rescue program.

Text copyright © 2023 by Lynne Cox

Jacket and interior illustrations copyright © 2023 by Richard Jones

All rights reserved. Published in the United States by Anne Schwartz Books,
an imprint of Random House Children's Books,
a division of Penguin Random House LLC, New York.

Anne Schwartz Books and the colophon are trademarks of Penguin Random House LLC.

Visit us on the Web! rhcbooks.com
Educators and librarians, for a variety of teaching tools, visit us at RHTeachersLibrarians.com

Library of Congress Cataloging-in-Publication Data is available upon request.
ISBN 978-0-593-42568-8 (trade) — ISBN 978-0-593-42569-5 (lib. bdg.) — ISBN 978-0-593-42570-1 (ebook)

The text of this book is set in 15-point Goudy Sans.
The illustrations were rendered in paint and edited in Adobe Photoshop.
Book design by Sarah Hokanson

MANUFACTURED IN CHINA
10 9 8 7 6 5 4 3 2   First Edition

Yoshi

Sea Turtle Genius

A True Story About an Amazing Swimmer

by Lynne Cox

illustrated by Richard Jones

a·s·b

anne schwartz books

Inside the egg was genius.

The tiny loggerhead turtle cracked through her shell, stuck her head out, and pushed the pieces aside. She was just the size of a smile.

For days, the baby turtle stayed under the sand in a nest on a beach in Australia, with her many brothers and sisters.

Then, near midnight on the fifth night, when the sand was cool and the tide was high, the turtle pulled herself out. She felt the force of the earth. She smelled the air and saw the shimmering reflections of the moon and stars on the water. And she used all of this to find her way down to the Indian Ocean.

From the shadows, ghost crabs and red foxes began to attack.
The baby turtle scrambled furiously to the water, along with her siblings.
When a huge wave picked her up, she took a deep breath and dove under.

For the first time in her new life, the little turtle was swimming. She glided over Mermaid Reef, her front flippers folded against her tiny brown shell and her back flippers kicking.

Below her lay an extraordinary world.

Seahorses rode currents among slender green sea grass. Clown fish chased butterfly fish. Soft sea anemones spread their tentacles, and parrotfish fed on algae.

A whale shark as big as a school bus swam by, wagging his body from side to side, mouth wide open to catch tiny plants and sea animals.

All night and day the tiny turtle swam without stopping, until she reached a raft of brown algae. She climbed on, hidden from hungry seabirds and fish.

For many months, the turtle drifted on algae pushed by strong sea currents and swam all alone across the wide Indian Ocean. Her beautiful shell turned reddish brown and grew into the shape of a heart.

After five years, the turtle, who was now the size of a house cat, reached the southern tip of Africa. She swam with penguins, fur seals, bottlenose dolphins, great white sharks, and yellow-bellied sea snakes. She dove between waving sea fans and squishy yellow sponges and hunted for crabs and clams and mussels.

In the surf, she watched baboons chasing each other down the beach, zebras wading in the shallows, and ostriches walking along the shore.

The turtle moved slowly, searching
for food. When she reached deeper
water, she took a big breath and dove.

A fish trapped in a net
caught her attention.

Into the net she swam and
immediately became tangled.

She needed to get to
the surface to breathe,
or she would drown.

The net pulled tighter.

The harder she tried to
break free, the more tangled
she became.

Slowly, the turtle inched her way up and up and up through the water, dragging the net with her. At last she broke through the surface! But she could not rest. The net was weighing her down.

For hours, the turtle treaded water, trying to poke her
head out for air, growing more and more exhausted.
In the vast ocean, she was just a dot.

But then the turtle's luck changed. A fisherman saw her struggling.

He pulled the net into his boat and took the turtle in his hands. He felt her pulse racing. He cut the net off with his knife as he spoke to her gently, telling her not to be afraid.

At last the turtle was free.

But there was a gash on one side of her shell. The fisherman knew she would need immediate treatment or she would die.

He placed a towel over her eyes to calm her, removed the broken pieces of shell, bathed her with fresh water to kill any parasites, and put antiseptic on her wound.

Over the next months, the fisherman cared for the turtle while her shell healed. He fed her squid and she grew stronger. He named her Yoshi, which means "good luck" in Japanese.

Before heading home to Japan, the fisherman brought Yoshi to Two Oceans Aquarium in Cape Town, South Africa. The aquarium's curator and veterinarian had no experience caring for a sea turtle. Still, they worried that Yoshi may have become tame during her time with the fisherman and would not be able to survive in the wild. They decided to keep her.

For over twenty years, Yoshi lived at the aquarium. She grew to the size of a lion in a tank she shared with ragged-tooth sharks, yellow tail flash fish, giant kob, schools of garrick, and stingrays. Sea turtles are not social animals. Yoshi did not pay attention to the others, but there were divers she liked to follow.

Yoshi was now an adult sea turtle. The curator, veterinarian, and animal behaviorists decided she was ready to return to her natural habitat, the ocean. But she had spent so many years in a tank! How could she swim the great distances necessary for a turtle to survive?

To get Yoshi into shape, two divers positioned themselves on either side of the tank. Back and forth, back and forth she swam between them—sixty-five feet each way. At the end of each workout, she was fed a bite of crab as a treat.

Yoshi trained every day for eighteen months, building up her strength and endurance until she became a powerful swimmer.

MOP22

Before they released her, scientists attached a tracking device to Yoshi's shell so they could follow her by satellite. She was so heavy that it took a group to lift her over the side of the boat and gently lower her into the sea. At last she was returning to her natural home.

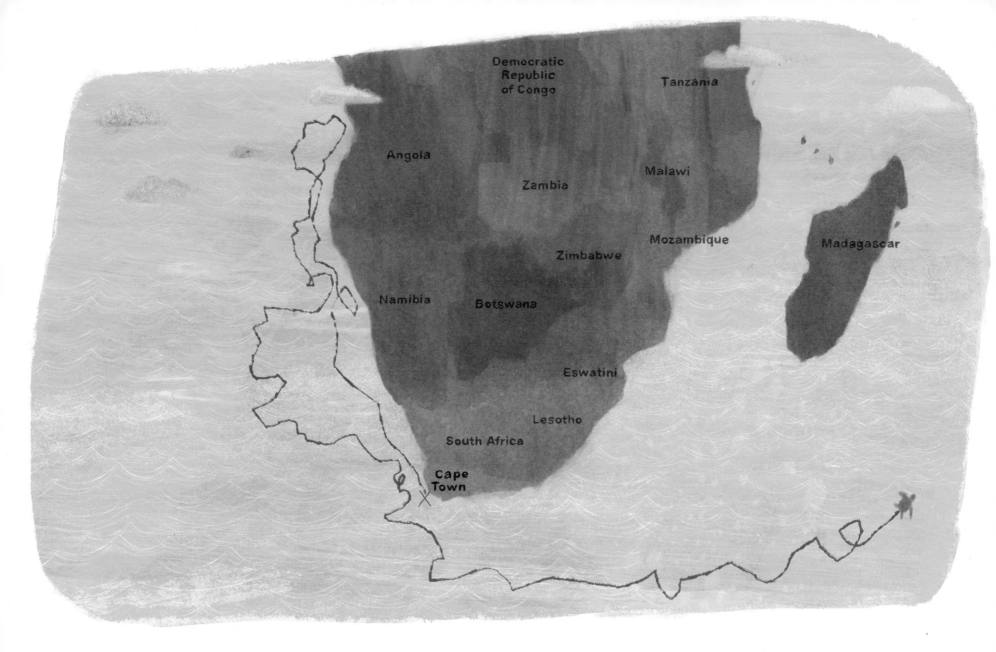

Yoshi swam up the west coast of South Africa, along the shores of Namibia and Angola, where there was plenty of food. Then she turned and swam back around the tip of Africa. Scientists thought she was heading to the nearest loggerhead nesting site, 2,174 miles north of Cape Town—until she did something no one expected. She began swimming across the Indian Ocean toward Australia.

Children and adults from all over the globe followed her progress on their computers. Where was Yoshi going?

Yoshi swam more than thirty miles each day. She swam through giant waves and across calm seas. She swam through huge storms and bright sunny days. She floated half asleep through the night. Her body glowed in a blanket of sparkling water that looked magical in the moonlight.

She felt the force of the earth. She felt the call in her heart.

She fought the currents, the tides, and the winds. She swam through summer, fall, winter, and spring, and she kept going. She swam 22,998 miles in twenty-six months all the way to Mermaid Reef Marine Park in Australia, setting the record for the longest swim of any animal in history.

On the reef, a male loggerhead turtle saw Yoshi and swam to her. They mated.

A few months later, guided by the smell of the sand, Yoshi crawled from the water onto the beach where she had been born twenty-five years earlier.

Yoshi found her way home.

And then she laid eggs on that same beach.
Somehow Yoshi knew. There was genius inside her.

And inside each egg was genius.

Author's Note

Yoshi is a real turtle whose remarkable journey has captivated people around the world. Though I imagined Yoshi's life before she was caught in the fisherman's net, everything else in this story is true. At

Jean Tresfon

first, scientists believed that she was born on a beach 2,174 miles north of Cape Town, South Africa, where there was a large loggerhead nesting site, but when they released her, Yoshi surprised them. Instead of swimming north, she swam west. Like all sea turtles, Yoshi sensed the invisible lines of the earth's magnetic field in the water, and she used them to navigate across the Indian Ocean all the way to Australia. The scientists realized that this was where she had come from. Yoshi now lives off the coast of Western Australia. She is still being tracked by satellite, and scientists and people around the globe continue to follow her.

A female sea turtle digs a nest in the sand, then lays her eggs and covers them. The eggs incubate and become baby sea turtles. If the temperature in the nest is above 87.8 degrees Fahrenheit, the babies will be female, and if it is below 81.86 degrees Fahrenheit, they will be male. If the temperature fluctuates, there will be a mix of female and male turtles. Only one or two baby loggerheads out of 1,000 hatchlings survive to maturity, but those turtles that do can live up to one hundred years.

Loggerhead turtles are on the endangered species list and are at serious risk of becoming extinct. There are groups around the world working to protect the turtles' nesting sites. Organizations such as Two Oceans Aquarium are rehabilitating injured sea turtles like Yoshi and teaching people about this amazing and beautiful animal.

I am intrigued by Yoshi's story because I too am a long-distance swimmer. I was the first person to swim around the rough waters surrounding the Cape of Good Hope, Africa. I was amazed that Yoshi swam thousands of miles from Africa to Australia and that she found the beach where she was born. I also spent time in Playa Hermosa, Costa Rica, at the Sea Turtle Refuge. I helped watch over sea turtles hatching and was inspired by the power and determination within each little turtle to get down the beach and into the ocean.

Map of Yoshi's record swim

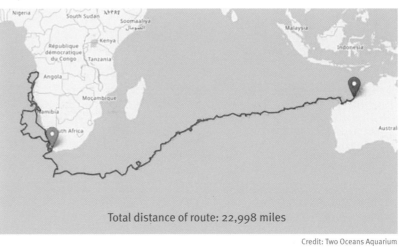

Total distance of route: 22,998 miles

Credit: Two Oceans Aquarium

To learn more about Yoshi, visit:

youtube.com/watch?v=4ESgbWTJuGA&feature=emb_rel_end

aquarium.co.za/blog/entry/yoshi-has-reached-australia-record-breaking-turtles -long-distance

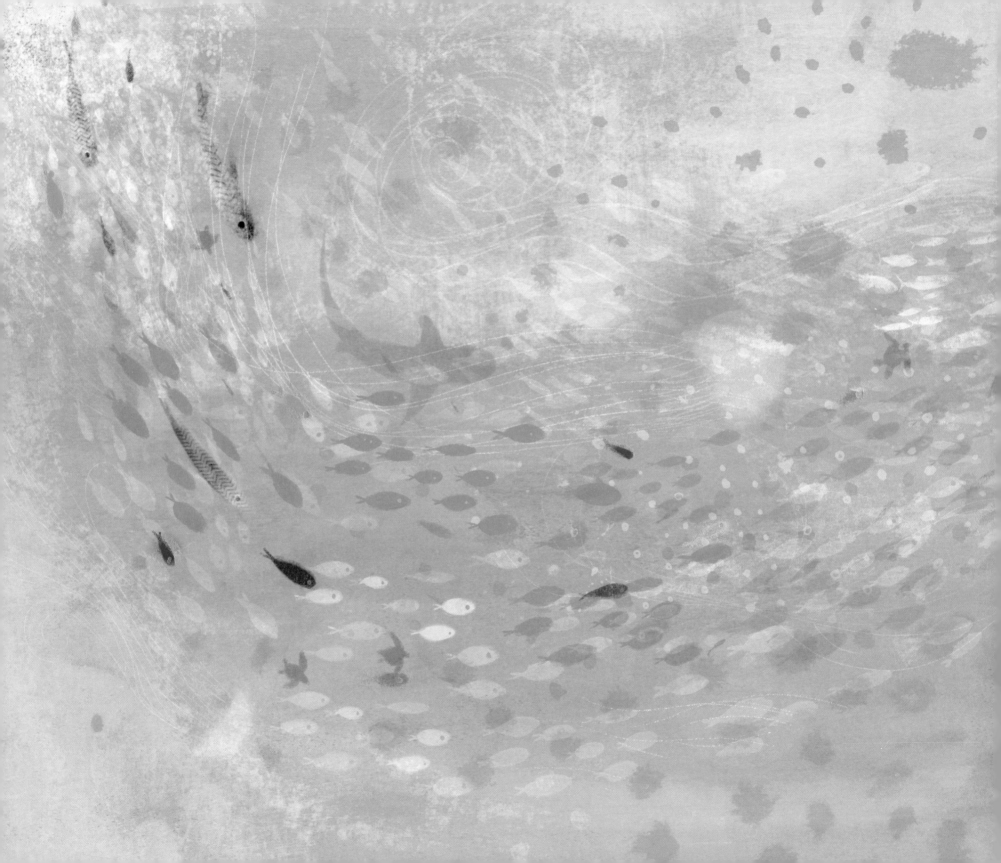